LISA McGEE

Originally from Derry, Northern Ireland, Lisa read Drama at
Queens University, Belfast. She was writer on attachment at the
Royal National Theatre, London, in 2006. Her plays include
Girls and Dolls (Stewart Parker Award Winner, Susan Smith
Blackburn Prize runner-up, Irish Theatre Award nominee);
Jump! (Exchange Theatre, New York); *Seven Years and Seven
Hours* (Rough Magic Theatre Company, Dublin); and *The
Young Man with the Cream Tarts* (Sneaky Productions, Belfast).
Television includes *The Things I Haven't Told You* (Tiger
Aspect/BBC); *Totally Frank* (Endemol/Channel4).

Lisa is creator and lead writer of the IFTA award-winning series
Raw (Ecosse/RTÉ). She is currently working on a film
adaptation of her play *Jump!* (NI Screen/Hotshot Films), season
two of *Raw*, and a new television series in development.

Other Titles in this Series

Jez Butterworth
MOJO
THE NIGHT HERON
PARLOUR SONG
THE WINTERLING

Caryl Churchill
BLUE HEART
CHURCHILL PLAYS: THREE
CHURCHILL PLAYS: FOUR
CHURCHILL: SHORTS
CLOUD NINE
A DREAM PLAY *after* Strindberg
DRUNK ENOUGH TO SAY
    I LOVE YOU?
FAR AWAY
HOTEL
ICECREAM
LIGHT SHINING IN
    BUCKINGHAMSHIRE
MAD FOREST
A NUMBER
SEVEN JEWISH CHILDREN
THE SKRIKER
THIS IS A CHAIR
THYESTES *after* Seneca
TRAPS

Stella Feehily
DUCK
O GO MY MAN

Declan Feenan
ST PETERSBURG and other plays

debbie tucker green
BORN BAD
DIRTY BUTTERFLY
RANDOM
STONING MARY
TRADE & GENERATIONS

Joel Horwood
FOOD *with* Christopher Heimann
I CAUGHT CRABS
    IN WALBERSWICK
STOOPUD FUCKEN ANIMALS

Lucy Kirkwood
HEDDA *after* Ibsen
TINDERBOX

Owen McCafferty
ANTIGONE *after* Sophocles
CLOSING TIME
DAYS OF WINE AND ROSES
    after JP Miller
MOJO MICKYBO
SHOOT THE CROW
SCENES FROM THE
    BIG PICTURE

Ian McHugh
HOW TO CURSE

Conor McPherson
DUBLIN CAROL
McPHERSON: FOUR PLAYS
McPHERSON PLAYS: TWO
PORT AUTHORITY
THE SEAFARER
SHINING CITY
THE WEIR

Chloë Moss
CHRISTMAS IS MILES AWAY
HOW LOVE IS SPELT
THIS WIDE NIGHT
THE WAY HOME

Mark O'Rowe
FROM BOTH HIPS &
    THE ASPIDISTRA CODE
HOWIE THE ROOKIE
MADE IN CHINA
TERMINUS

Ali Taylor
COTTON WOOL
OVERSPILL

Jack Thorne
STACY & FANNY AND FAGGOT
WHEN YOU CURE ME

Enda Walsh
BEDBOUND & MISTERMAN
DELIRIUM
DISCO PIGS & SUCKING
    DUBLIN
THE NEW ELECTRIC BALLROM
THE SMALL THINGS
THE WALWORTH FARCE

Lisa McGee

GIRLS AND DOLLS

NICK HERN BOOKS

London

www.nickhernbooks.co.uk

A Nick Hern Book

Girls and Dolls first published in this version in Great Britain as a paperback original in 2006 by Nick Hern Books Limited, 14 Larden Road, London W3 7ST

Reprinted in this revised version 2009

Girls and Dolls copyright © 2006, 2009 Lisa McGee

Lisa McGee has asserted her right to be identified as the author of this work

Cover photograph by Robert Malone
Front cover image design by Nu Design, Belfast
Cover design by Ned Hoste, 2H

Typeset by Nick Hern Books, London
Printed and bound in Great Britain by CPI Antony Rowe, Chippenham, Wiltshire

A CIP catalogue record for this book is available from the British Library

ISBN   978 1 85459 970 4

FSC
Mixed Sources
Product group from well-managed
forests and other controlled sources

Cert no. SGS-COC-2953
www.fsc.org
© 1996 Forest Stewardship Council

Girls and Dolls was first produced by Tinderbox Theatre
Company at the Drama and Film Centre at Queens University,
Belfast, on 9 November 2006, followed by a tour, with the
following cast:

YOUNG CLARE   Bernadette Brown
ADULT CLARE   Mary Jordan
YOUNG EMMA   Sarah Lyle
ADULT EMMA   Veronica Leer

Director   Michael Duke
Dramaturg   Hannah Slättne
Designer   Terry Laine
Lighting Designer   Patrick McLaughlin

This revised version of the play was produced by
paper/scissors/stone at the Old Red Lion, London, on 3
February 2009, with the following cast:

CLARE   Niamh McGrady
EMMA   Bronágh Taggart

Director   Derek Bond
Designer   James Perkins
Lighting Designer   Sally Ferguson

For my parents

Characters

The play is intended for two female actors:

CLARE, *thirties*
EMMA, *thirties*

*These main characters move frequently and effortlessly between
their child and adult voices. All characters are represented
through their eyes. The following roles should be divided as
follows:*

FIRST ACTOR (CLARE)	SECOND ACTOR (EMMA)
YOUNG CLARE	YOUNG EMMA
MAGS	MR RICE
DENNIS	CONNOR'S MOTHER
RITA	JOSIE
PRIEST	MARTY
CASPER	LOVELY LAURA
SWEET PETE	CLARE'S FATHER
EMMA'S FATHER	CLARE'S MOTHER
EMMA'S MOTHER	IRA MAN 1
SARAH	DERVLA
TANK	
IRA MAN 2	

CLARE *and* EMMA *sit on two chairs facing the audience*.

CLARE. Sometimes I think this is pointless. Sometimes I think I have nothing to add.

EMMA. When it's already been recorded.

CLARE. All factually correct.

EMMA. In solid, sober black and white.

CLARE. But that's not how it seemed.

EMMA. I can go back there in an instant.

CLARE. It was bright.

EMMA. In a second.

CLARE. And it buzzed.

EMMA. To start with… In the beginning.

CLARE. To begin, introduce, initiate, activate.

EMMA. It's best, I suppose, to find a point.

CLARE. Establish, launch, instigate, originate.

EMMA. And then to move on.

CLARE. To start.

EMMA. That year would be the obvious one.

CLARE. Other things happened that year.

EMMA. When John-Paul praying at Knock was still fresh, still real.

CLARE. Ireland *Semper Fidelis*.

EMMA. Had only slipped into the recent past, like yesterday or the day before.

CLARE. But despite his appearance we found ourselves still surrounded by bad men, bad men in uniforms, bad men in redundant camouflage, there were even bad men among us. And at the head of it all, at the pinnacle, a very bad woman.

EMMA. The lady was not for turning.

CLARE. For it's as simple as that, isn't it? Good and bad. Right and wrong.

EMMA. It was the year of the Rubik's Cube.

CLARE. When Blondie were non-movers.

EMMA. The year JR got shot.

CLARE. And Mark Chapman pulled his trigger.

EMMA. When we all, in secret, gathered in some faceless person's living room, glued to a screen, petrified, frozen, delighted.

CLARE. Here's Johnny!

EMMA. It all was that.

CLARE. I can go back.

EMMA. It can be triggered by the strangest things.

CLARE. I had my dream again.

EMMA. Vanilla musk, fruit-shaped soaps, shit cartoons.

CLARE. I'm standing there, in that street.

EMMA. Fifty-two terraced houses facing fifty-two more.

CLARE. Only the pavements are gold, the bricks are made of gold.

EMMA. My hair hanging around my face.

CLARE. The sky is bright blue.

EMMA. Trying to shake a stone from my shoe.

CLARE. And she's there.

EMMA. My knees all covered in scabs that I'd been told not to pick.

CLARE. Of course, she would be.

EMMA. Apparently someone once lost a leg that way.

CLARE. We were inseparable.

EMMA. And then there was her.

CLARE. They always said you didn't see one without the other.

EMMA. Since the day we met.

CLARE. I can never remember the actual day.

EMMA. We met at the swings.

CLARE. It might have been at the park.

EMMA. In the park.

CLARE. It wasn't very good.

EMMA. It was terrible.

CLARE. The slide didn't work.

EMMA. You would always get stuck halfway down.

CLARE. Maybe it was the rain.

EMMA. It rained a lot, you see.

CLARE. The park keeper was…

EMMA. A nice enough man.

CLARE. A creep.

EMMA. His name was Jim.

CLARE. John… something.

EMMA. When he walked he kind of dragged his feet.

CLARE. Because he had a limp.

EMMA. Because his boots didn't fit him properly.

CLARE. I think he was an alcoholic.

EMMA. Someone once told me he was a Protestant.

CLARE. I could be wrong.

EMMA. He tried his best to keep it tidy, the park.

CLARE. He did nothing.

EMMA. It wasn't easy.

CLARE. Except throw us out so he could lock up early.

EMMA. The older boys liked to burn things. A lot.

CLARE. But we would always sneak back in.

EMMA. Under the railings.

CLARE. Over the railings. Was that were we met?

EMMA. That's where I saw her for the first time.

CLARE. It's possible. I definitely remember an incident there. In the beginning. (*Pause.*) Once upon a time.

EMMA. She was sitting on my swing.

CLARE. She said I stole it.

EMMA. She asked me if my name was on it.

CLARE. It wasn't.

EMMA. I said she couldn't sit there.

CLARE. I told her it was a free country…

EMMA. This was a valid argument, I suppose.

CLARE. I don't think she gave my point much consideration.

The Park

EMMA. Move.

CLARE. No.

EMMA. Now!

CLARE. No.

EMMA. It's mine.

CLARE. Says who?

EMMA. Says me.

CLARE. And who the fuck are you?

EMMA. You said fuck.

CLARE. So did you.

EMMA (*gasps*). Bitch!

CLARE. Takes one to know one.

EMMA. Is that the best you can do?

CLARE. I'm not moving.

EMMA. You better.

CLARE. Or what?

EMMA. Or I'll do it for you.

CLARE. You will.

EMMA. I will.

CLARE. Aye, right.

EMMA. I'm warning you.

CLARE. I'm shaking.

EMMA. I'm gonna hit you a slap.

CLARE. Go then.

EMMA. I'm serious.

CLARE. I dare you.

EMMA. Do you now?

CLARE. This went on for some time.

EMMA. It was starting to get boring.

CLARE. But I stood my ground, or rather kept swinging in the air.

EMMA. It reached the stage where I had to do something.

CLARE. She pushed me.

EMMA. She hit the ground with a thump.

CLARE. I hurt my head.

EMMA. She was just lying there in the gravel.

CLARE. You psycho.

EMMA. Are you okay?

CLARE. Do I look okay?

EMMA. Kind of.

CLARE. I'm bleeding! From my head! Look my head's bleeding.

EMMA. No, you've scratched your hand, the blood's coming from your hand.

CLARE. You're mental.

EMMA. Look, calm down.

CLARE. Pure mental, pure basket case.

EMMA. I'm sorry, I'm sorry about your han... head. You wouldn't move.

CLARE. You could have just asked me.

EMMA. What? I did ask you.

CLARE. Aye, well, that's not what I'll be telling my ma.

EMMA. But that's not the truth.

CLARE. I'm probably scarred for life.

EMMA. Don't tell your ma.

CLARE. Aye, cos I'm gonna do what you want.

EMMA. She'll tell my ma.

CLARE. She doesn't know your ma.

EMMA. She'll find her; they can always find each other.

CLARE. Why should I care what happens to you?

EMMA. I'm sorry.

CLARE. Of course you're sorry now.

EMMA. My ma says if I hit anyone else she's sending me to
live with my granda.

CLARE. And what?

EMMA. My granda's dead.

Pause.

CLARE. My ma always threatens to send me to her sister
Kathy's. Aunt Kathy's mad. She thinks she can speak in
tongues.

EMMA. Like Jesus?

CLARE. Aye... a bit like Jesus.

EMMA. Don't tell anybody. You won't, will you? I didn't mean
it, I swear.

CLARE. I won't if...

EMMA. If what?

CLARE. I won't if from now on this is my swing.

EMMA. And that was that a deal was made and peace was
restored.

CLARE. A good job too.

EMMA. She turned up in my class shortly after that.

CLARE. The new girl.

EMMA. Mr Rice taught us then.

CLARE. I liked him.

School

MR RICE. Everyone, this is Clare. Clare, this is everyone. Clare's just moved from St Patrick's…

CLARE. St John's.

MR RICE. I was told St Patrick's.

CLARE. No. St John's.

MR RICE. You're sure?

CLARE. I was there for five years, sir.

MR RICE. Right. Of course you were. Clare's just moved from St John's. I know you'll all make her feel very welcome. Do you know anyone in the class, Clare?

CLARE. Sort of.

MR RICE. Who?

CLARE. Her.

EMMA. She pointed at me. Mr Rice made Connor move so she could sit beside me. I was glad; Connor smelt of piss and sometimes tried to feel my leg.

CLARE. We sat together like that the whole year. Mr Rice was brilliant. Like no one else I knew. Blunt and to the point but brilliant nonetheless. If he caught someone writing on their desk he'd say…

MR RICE. Would you do that in your own house?

CLARE. Or if someone was whispering…

MR RICE. Would you like to share it with the rest of the class?

CLARE. And on rare occasions…

MR RICE. Are you trying to fuck with me, boy?

CLARE. These questions were mostly rhetorical but sometimes Connor would try to answer them. Connor was an asshole.

Mr Rice said that when he was born they threw away the child and raised the afterbirth. He was sent home from school one day because of the smell. Mr Rice told him to have a wash. He returned unwashed with a note from his mother.

CONNOR'S MOTHER. Dear Mr Rice, Connor tells me you sent him home from school today because he smelt. I send my son to school to be teached, not to be smelt – he's not a rose, you know.

CLARE. Connor's torture continued. The summer was awful, we had to keep all the windows open.

EMMA. It was great, running around trying to swat all the wasps and bees that flew in, a welcome distraction from what we were supposed to be doing.

CLARE. Did my head in.

EMMA. She was clever; she was good at nearly everything. In practice tests we would always finish at the same time, her because she'd done it all in half an hour, me because I never knew where to start.

CLARE. We read *Animal Farm*.

EMMA. It wasn't too bad.

CLARE. I've read it lots of times since. We were told it was the best book ever written.

MR RICE. If you learn anything from me, boys and girls, let it be this: One – *Animal Farm* is the best book ever written. Two – The Rolling Stones are the best band of all time. And three – Teaching is the worst profession in the world.

CLARE. And I generally believed whatever he said. Even though I've yet to meet someone who broke their back due to swinging on a chair, who lost their arm whilst waving out a bus window or who took someone's eye out by being care-less with a ruler.

EMMA. And then one day he was just gone.

CLARE. He didn't say he was going.

EMMA. He didn't get a chance.

CLARE. We just came in one day and that fucking witch was sitting in his chair.

EMMA. Miss Ryder.

CLARE. Nobody would ride her. Cunt.

EMMA. Apparently, Connor the smelly bastard had been acting up in the corridor. Mr Rice said that he would knock seven shades of shit out of him. Miss Ryder overheard this and that was that. He was asked to leave.

CLARE. He wouldn't really have done it.

EMMA. Miss Ryder didn't say shit or fuck; if you misbehaved she stood you in the corner or sent you home. She read interior-design magazines; she made us do all the textbook exercises.

CLARE. School was never the same after that. It was boring, pointless.

EMMA. I wonder what he's doing now.

CLARE. He had to write a report about us at the time.

EMMA. He didn't do any interviews.

CLARE. Miss Ryder did lots.

EMMA. We played outside most of that summer.

CLARE. In the street.

EMMA. The usual stuff.

CLARE. Out pops one, out pops two, out pops another one...

EMMA. And that meant me.

CLARE. She was always it.

EMMA. Running wasn't my strong point.

CLARE. It made me laugh.

EMMA. Skipping was.

CLARE. Cinderella dressed in yella, went upstairs to meet her fella.

EMMA. Hide-and-seek, knick-knock, footballs, tennis balls, hula hoops, marbles, roller boots, elastics…

CLARE. Anything at all.

EMMA. Just normal. Just what we knew.

CLARE. We would go messages.

EMMA. It was a nice little earner.

CLARE. Keep the change.

EMMA. My mother said I was a good wee businesswoman.

CLARE. Our best clients.

EMMA. At the time.

CLARE. Lived in number 24.

EMMA. Mags and –

CLARE. What was the other one's name?

EMMA. Josie.

CLARE. I can't remember her name. They were…

EMMA. Old.

CLARE. Sisters.

EMMA. I'm not sure what age exactly.

CLARE. Never married.

EMMA. But they seemed like ancient relics.

CLARE. They knew everything.

EMMA. About everyone. The wicked witches of the east and west.

CLARE. They always needed things.

EMMA. From the shop.

Outside Mags and Josie's House

MAGS. What do I need now, let me think now, what was it I said I needed? Maybe I should write you a list, love.

CLARE. No, it's grand, Mags, just tell me, I'll remember – and if I don't Emma will.

MAGS. Ach, you're a good girl. She's a good girl, isn't she, Josie?

JOSIE. She is surely. She's a lovely girl, a lovely well-man-nered girl. It's a miracle when you look at that father of hers, if ever there was an ignorant, stuck-up aul'...

MAGS. I think we need milk.

JOSIE. How's your mammy keeping, Emma?

MAGS. And we should probably get some biscuits as well. Will you remember this?

CLARE. Yeah, I'll remember.

EMMA. Aye, she's grand. I think.

CLARE. I have a really good memory. Mr Rice said it was retentive.

MAGS. Really? Dr White says my water's retentive.

JOSIE. Ach, she doesn't have it easy either now, does she? Sickness is no joke; it's no joke at all. I can tell you that. Get me fags as well, Maggie.

MAGS. No bother, but first I need to run out to that tree in the back garden.

JOSIE. What tree?

MAGS. You know, the one all the money grows on.

JOSIE. Don't be such a tight aul' bitch, I'll give you it back.

MAGS. That's right, girls, Josie's waiting on a cheque coming in for a bit of modelling work she's been doing.

CLARE. Dennis said he's not serving us fags any more.

EMMA. Oh aye, that's right, he doesn't want us buying fags any more.

JOSIE. Doesn't want you buying fags? Sure, you're only wains.

MAGS. I think that's his point.

JOSIE. Ach, that's ridiculous.

MAGS. You'll just have to get up off your fat arse and get them yourself.

JOSIE. Up that hill! Are you mad? I'm not well.

MAGS. Oh aye, that's right. Walking kills.

JOSIE. Just tell Dennis they're for me. I'm away to get my purse. Hold on there two seconds.

MAGS. Hurry up. I need milk for my tea. I've a mouth on me like Ghandi's flip-flop.

CLARE. They're dead now, the both of them. They must be.

EMMA. I heard that Mags died first. My mother told me, at her wake, someone asked Josie if she took sugar in her tea, She said she didn't know, Mags always made the tea.

The Shop

CLARE. Dennis O'Donnell's shop was brilliant.

EMMA. Part newsagent, part bakery, part hardware, part chemist.

CLARE. He even hired videos.

EMMA. Specialising in two specific genres.

CLARE. Crap sequels.

EMMA. And badly pirated new releases.

CLARE. We'd seen then all. Twice.

EMMA. Though ours fitted neither category.

CLARE. Back wall, bottom shelf, left-hand side.

EMMA. It was old. Really old.

CLARE. We'd take it back to hers and watch it.

EMMA. She liked it. She said it was her favourite film.

CLARE. Over and over again.

EMMA. I knew all the words.

CLARE. The Emerald City, the Scarecrow, the Tin Man, the Cowardly Lion and of course old Judy, leading the way.

EMMA. Toto, I don't think we're in Kansas any more.

CLARE. I wanted that. I wanted to skip down the Yellow Brick Road. I'd have given anything, an escape.

EMMA. An adventure.

CLARE. She was so stupid, Dorothy. I always thought she was so stupid. Look at where she was and all she could think about was going home. Going back to her boring black-and-white home. I would think to myself, stay there; stay there with the talking trees and the flying monkeys. I would. I wouldn't even be scared. I'd live there. I'd never come back. I'd live in the Emerald City with all my friends and I'd be happy. We would pray for a twister. Hearing a strong wind I'd run outside, looking up at the sky, hoping, waiting. One never came.

EMMA. My mother said there wasn't much call for twisters. My mother said we had enough of bother.

CLARE. When we were in town, we'd try on every pair of red shoes we saw, regardless of size or shape, just in case.

EMMA. Click, click, click. There's no place like Oz.

CLARE. I always wanted a pair of red shoes.

EMMA. My father said it was unlikely the ruby slippers would turn up in the Doohan's half-price sale. My father said we were ejeets. (*Beat.*) As a shopkeeper, Dennis was a bit of a natural.

DENNIS. What the fuck did I tell you about wearing them fucking roller boots in my fucking shop? Out to fuck.

EMMA. He provided a speedy service.

DENNIS. Am I running a museum here? Am I? Buy and go. Buy and go. 'Just looking' doesn't pay my rent.

EMMA. The thrill of stealing from Dennis O'Donnell lay in the fact that if he caught you, he would actually kill you.

CLARE. We never got caught.

EMMA. He, we were told, buried would-be criminals in his front garden. That was why roses grew there. Well-fertilised soil.

CLARE. We were cleverer than most.

EMMA. It was pure luck really.

CLARE. We were always buying, you see, for Josie or Mags or someone, so...

EMMA. While I was paying.

CLARE. While I was paying.

EMMA. She would steal.

CLARE. She would steal.

EMMA. She didn't need to. She always had money.

CLARE. I couldn't spend it.

EMMA. He always gave her money.

CLARE. Too much.

EMMA. I was so jealous.

CLARE. Counting our takings from O'Donnell's shop was always a good way to spend the afternoon.

The Street

EMMA. Three packets of crisps.

CLARE. I don't like cheese and onion.

EMMA. He keeps the salt and vinegar too high up.

CLARE. I know. You can have them.

EMMA. A can of Coke.

CLARE. A tomato.

EMMA. The *Daily Mirror*.

CLARE. A toothbrush.

EMMA. Air freshener.

CLARE. A packet of water balloons.

EMMA. No way!

CLARE. Look. (*Shows her.*)

EMMA. I always thought he kept those behind the counter.

CLARE. He does.

EMMA. You're mad.

CLARE. I'm brilliant.

EMMA. What if he had turned round?

CLARE. He didn't. Did he?

EMMA. You'd have been dead.

CLARE. But I'm not dead, I'm here, and I have a packet of water balloons.

EMMA. We need to put all these in your house.

CLARE. I want to go to the park.

EMMA. We can't carry all this stuff to the park.

CLARE. Why my house?

EMMA. My ma is starting to twig, I think.

CLARE. We can just throw them away.

EMMA. Then what's the point? What's the point in taking them?

CLARE. There is no point.

EMMA. I'm not throwing this stuff away.

CLARE. All we want is the water balloons.

EMMA. I want all of it. I think we should keep it all. Everything. And then when we have enough, we can open our own shop.

CLARE. Okay, we'll go to my house and put it all in my room, but then we're going straight to the park.

EMMA. We're always in the park. We never play in your room.

CLARE. We're going straight to the park.

EMMA. Why?

CLARE. I said so. That's why.

EMMA. Her room was great.

CLARE. Full of crap.

EMMA. It was like a toyshop.

CLARE. Oh, they had a field day with that.

EMMA. Everything. She had everything.

CLARE. I discovered there was something worse than a monster. A spoilt one.

EMMA. No one else had toys like those. But she never liked to stay there long. God, I used to hate her.

CLARE. I liked being outside.

EMMA. I remember he bought her this doll.

CLARE. Stupid thing.

EMMA. You should have seen it.

CLARE. Ridiculous thing.

EMMA. You put this key in its back and you could make it cry
and crawl and it took a bottle, and wet its nappy. Amazing. I
asked my mother if I could have one. She said it would probably be cheaper for her just to have another child.

CLARE. I never wanted it.

EMMA. She cut off all its hair.

CLARE. She was shouting, 'No! No! Give it to me!'

EMMA. Drew on its face.

CLARE. 'I want it. I'll take it.'

EMMA. Then she stood on its back.

CLARE. She couldn't have it.

EMMA. Jumped on its back.

CLARE. It was stupid, annoying.

EMMA. Until it broke.

CLARE. Nobody could play with it after that.

EMMA. She never really explained herself.

CLARE. I didn't like dolls much.

CLARE. I hated Saturdays. She was never around.

EMMA. I nearly always spent Saturday with my Auntie Rita.

CLARE. I'm not sure which one she was.

EMMA. My mammy's oldest sister.

CLARE. There were always lots of them running in and out.

EMMA. I didn't mind.

CLARE. Full of people, full of noise.

EMMA. She was good to me.

Aunt Rita's House

RITA. Right, love, you may take that top off till I give it a wee iron, for you're like a walking wrinkle. Then we'll sit down, have our dinner, watch a bit of TV…

EMMA. Sometimes she'd piss me off.

RITA. Sure, then we can go to mass.

EMMA. Ach, do we have to?

RITA. Don't start now, Emma love.

EMMA. It's boring.

RITA. Boring! It's not boring. How's it boring? Don't be so silly. Sure, doesn't there be singing and stories and magic?

EMMA. Crap singing, crap stories and what magic?

RITA. Water into wine! Water into wine! No magic! Don't say crap.

EMMA. Ach, that's not real magic, Aunt Rita.

RITA. May God forgive you, young lady. You'll be making your confirmation next year. I don't know what your mother and father are playing at. Would you even go to mass at all if I wasn't here, I wonder?

EMMA. Well, when you were at Lourdes I never went for two weeks.

RITA. Isn't it a good job then that I had the knees prayed off myself? I just might have done enough for both of us.

EMMA. Mammy and Daddy slept in. It was brilliant.

RITA. I know your mother's not well, but you'd think that lazy brute she got married to would feel some sense of duty. Do you know what happens when wee girls don't go to mass? Our lady cries, and her tears make rain, and wee girls can't go out to play.

EMMA. You said that's what happens when wee girls swear.

RITA. She cries at different things. I'm your godmother; I'm responsible for you. If you aren't a good Catholic, when I die I'll go straight to hell, I'll be thrust into the burning flames of eternal damnation. Do you want your poor aunt to go to hell, Emma?

EMMA. No. No, of course I don't.

RITA. Good girl.

EMMA. God, I hated mass.

Mass

PRIEST. In the name of the Father, and of the Son, and of the Holy Spirit.

EMMA. My age, I suppose.

PRIEST. Amen.

EMMA. It made no sense, you know, to me.

PRIEST. You may be seated.

EMMA. There was always plenty to look at, though. My eyes would wander. Statues twice the size of me, and paintings that you would notice something different about on every visit. We'd always sit beside the one of Bernadette. Aunt Rita would say, 'Isn't she beautiful? Isn't she peaceful?' I never thought so, her stare drove right through me, I thought she looked insane, possessed. I zoned in and out, catching some words but never the meaning. Half listening. Half dreaming.

PRIEST. A reading from the letter of St John according to the Ritty Titty Tu Tu's.

EMMA. I wonder how the altar boys decide who gets to ring the bell.

PRIEST. This is the word of the Lord.

EMMA. They must take it in turns.

PRIEST. Honouring God and honouring the will of God.

EMMA. Maybe whoever's the oldest gets to do it.

PRIEST. It's not always easy in the world we live in today.

EMMA. That wouldn't really be fair, though.

PRIEST. Selfishness, lust, greed, depravity.

EMMA. Although the primary sevens get to do everything in school just because they're older. I hate the primary sevens.

PRIEST. Is this acceptable, just because it happens? Just because it exists, my friends, does not mean it's right. Does not mean it's what God intended.

EMMA. I'll be a primary seven in September.

PRIEST. There's people having sex outside of marriage and calling it 'making love'.

EMMA. Then I can boss people around.

PRIEST. Men having relations with other men and calling it 'gay'.

EMMA. Happy days. (*Pause*.) God, this is boring!

PRIEST. Committing adultery and calling it 'an affair'.

EMMA. I wonder has anyone ever actually died of boredom…

PRIEST. Watching filth and calling it 'entertainment'.

EMMA (*smiles*). I wonder does my Aunt Rita ever watch filth?

The Street

CLARE. When she wasn't there I had others, my standbys, my last resorts. There was her brother Marty and their cousin Casper. I didn't find them particularly stimulating.

MARTY. So then I kicked it right up against the shop window. Really hard, like.

CASPER. He did, right up against it. It nearly broke, so it did. The glass nearly broke it was (*Shows a small space between his thumb and finger.*) that close to breaking.

MARTY (*to* CASPER). Pack it in, dickwad, this is my story, I'm telling the story. (*Pause.*) So Dennis marches out. He was raging.

CASPER. You should have seen his face. Fucking raging.

MARTY. He had this baseball bat in his hands. Not a normal-sized baseball bat, like, this was a massive one.

CASPER. Fucking massive. Fucking huge. He was gonna kill us.

MARTY. Here, pasty-arse, pack it in, would ye! (*Pause.*) Then he shouts, 'Hey, did you just kick that ball against my window?' And I go, 'Aye, I did, what are you gonna do about it?' And he says, 'I'm gonna break both your fucking legs, that's what I'm gonna do about it. You'll not be playing football for a while, son.' And starts coming at me, with the bat.

CASPER. He did. He ran at him with it.

MARTY. He took a swing at me but I got a hold of it.

CASPER. Marty got the bat off him.

MARTY. I broke it in two, threw it at his feet and says to him, 'You'll not be doing much with it now, will you? You aul' bastard.'

CASPER. Swear to God.

MARTY. On my granny's grave.

CLARE. And there was lovely Laura. I don't think we liked Laura much.

LAURA. It's gonna be at the pool. It's a pool party. And there'll be a magician there. There's gonna be a whole entertainment area, with games and stuff and prizes. Proper prizes. Not like the ones at Louise Kerr's party, Mammy said they looked like they came out of Christmas crackers. No, mine will be all Barbie things. Barbie clothes, Barbie stationery, Barbie cars, Barbie pets, everything. And everyone's invited. Oh, except Emma. Mammy says she dresses like the homeless.

CLARE. But Peter was a different matter.

EMMA. Whatever happened to sweet Pete.

CLARE. We looked up to him. That little bit older. That little bit wiser.

EMMA. Without him I would never have found that place.

CLARE. He took her there, the first time.

EMMA. I wonder does that thought ever invade his mind?

CLARE. It's strange how everything's linked. Without this, there would be no that.

EMMA. I remember the trek. Knott's Wood. A fair walk when you've only got little legs. Maybe even a fair walk regardless. I wouldn't know. I've not been since. Pete led the way, pulling back branches and occasionally telling me to mind my step. It was no trouble for him. He glided through it, probably amused by my awkward stumbled progress. I was covered in red blotches from the stinging nettles.

Knott's Wood

PETE. Come on, Emma, keep up, not long now.

EMMA. Ah! Jesus! Bastard! Nettles!

PETE. Rub a wee dock leaf on your leg, Emma, you'll be grand.

EMMA. Bee! Bee! Giant fucking bee! (*Clasps her neck in pain*.)

PETE. I hope you're not allergic. I watched this programme about a fella who was allergic to bee stings. His body swoll out to three times its size, and then he died. At least I think he died. I didn't see the end.

EMMA. Pete, seriously... I'm starting to think there is no tree house. I'm starting to think you're a mentalist. That you've brought me here to kill me, and eat me.

PETE. Like a cannibal. I saw this programme about cannibals once...

EMMA. Where the fuck is it, Pete?

PETE (*looking up*). There you go, Emma, isn't it beautiful? Isn't it sweet?

EMMA. Is that it?

PETE. Dead right that's it.

EMMA. Why do you not want it any more?

PETE. It's not a question of wanting it. I'm fourteen now, you see, exams coming up and what not. I just don't have the time any more. Breaks my heart, like, it really does, but we all have to move on.

EMMA. How much?

PETE. Anyone else, a fiver; for you, three quid.

EMMA. Three pound! Pete, it's falling apart. It doesn't even have a ladder. And it's fucking miles away.

PETE. I'm not saying it isn't a bit of a fixer-upper, but the foundations are there... and as for location... well, you don't want your secret hideaway on your doorstep now, do you, Emma?

EMMA. I suppose... It might be a laugh fixing it up, it would give me and Clare something to do anyway.

CLARE. And it did give us something to do. All day. Every day. Have our breakfast, go to the tree house, home for lunch, then to the tree house. Dinner, tree house. We found a shortcut that even Pete hadn't known about. On each trip we brought something with us. Our stash from Dennis's shop, bits of furniture we'd lifted from the bonfire collection. Plates, cups, knives, forks and old bedclothes that we'd swiped from under our parents' noses. I wanted to live there. All the time. Never leave. I thought I could, because, ignoring the lack of electricity, heating and running water, it was perfect. A well-kept secret. I loved it. It was all I needed. To be up there. High up. Safe. My other world, my bubble, mine. Ours. (*Pause.*) I imagine myself there now, when I don't feel like facing it all. When I want to be all detached, all alone. You see, there are pieces I can keep, just for me. I think, let me wake up and be sitting there again. It never happens.

The Tree House

EMMA. Clare! Clare, wake up. Wake up, Clare.

CLARE (*confused*). What? What?

EMMA. You were sleeping.

CLARE. I don't know. What?

EMMA. You were sleeping.

CLARE. No, I wasn't. I just lay down. Just for a second.

EMMA. Have you been here all night?

CLARE. No. This morning. I came down this morning.

EMMA. Why didn't you call in for me?

CLARE. I woke up early. It was too early for you; you'd have still been in bed.

EMMA. You were supposed to help me bring Rita's old coffee table down. I couldn't lift it on my own, had to leave it behind.

CLARE. Sorry, okay? I'm sorry. We can get it later. Stop crying at me.

EMMA. I'm not crying at you. (*Pause.*) Do you come here other times without me?

CLARE. There's no rule, Emma, there's no law that says we always have to come here together.

EMMA. I know there isn't. I never said there was. I'm just wondering. I'm just asking.

CLARE. Well, I'm just answering.

Short silence.

We could stay here all night, you know. I mean, I didn't last night, but we could, if we wanted.

EMMA. I dunno. Do you think?

CLARE. Aye. Look at it.

EMMA. It does look brilliant… But it would be all dark and creepy here at night, there's nothing to sleep on either.

CLARE. On the floor, on our blankets.

EMMA. Naw. My ma and da would go mental if they twigged. So would yours.

CLARE. I don't care.

EMMA. Aye, right.

CLARE. What?

EMMA. You don't care.

CLARE. I don't. I don't give a fuck. What's the matter with you? You don't do anything.

EMMA. Aye, I do.

CLARE. What's wrong with you? You're so boring. Why are you so boring, Emma?

EMMA. Shut your mouth.

CLARE. Or what? What will you do? You're too chicken to do anything.

EMMA. I said shut up.

CLARE. You're just a wee dick, aren't you, Emma?

EMMA. I never said I wouldn't do it.

CLARE. That's what it sounded like to me.

EMMA. I'm not sleeping on the ground, all the insects will be crawling all over us. We'd need to get carpet or something.

CLARE. Then we'll get some.

EMMA. From where? Your living room?

The Shop

EMMA. We want to ask you something.

DENNIS. Ask me what? For my hand in marriage? Come on, girls. I have a business to run.

EMMA. It's about the rugs, the ones you sell down the back.

CLARE. We want the red one, you see.

EMMA. But we can't afford it.

DENNIS. Well, I think that's our conversation over then, isn't it? (*To another customer.*) Hi, fuck-features, you've been flicking through that paper for ten fucking minutes, do you want a pen and you can do the fucking crossword? (*Listens to customer's reply.*) Aye, too right you're buying it. (*Aside.*) Fuckwit.

EMMA (*nervously*). We were wondering, since no one ever buys them, if we could have one and pay up for it.

CLARE. Like in instalments. Every week or whatever.

EMMA. What do you think?

DENNIS. I think this is a corner shop not a catalogue. (*To the other customer.*) Or a fucking library.

EMMA. Or we have another idea. We could work it off. You know, the debt. Do chores for you and stuff.

DENNIS. Chores! Chores! What is this? *Little House on the* fucking *Prairie*?

EMMA. Do you watch *Little House on the Prairie*, Dennis?

DENNIS. Out. Now.

Emma's Living Room

EMMA. Hello, Daddy.

EMMA'S FATHER. Here, who's this? Who is this strange girl in my living room? I don't know her! What could she want with a poor man like me?

EMMA. Ach, Daddy, stop it.

EMMA'S FATHER. Why does she call me 'Daddy'? I did have a daughter once but she went out to play and never came back to visit her poor aul' father.

EMMA. Daddy, it's the summer, I have to go out and play.

EMMA'S FATHER. Emma, is that you?

EMMA. Pack it in; you know fine rightly it's me. (*Pause.*) Daddy?

EMMA'S FATHER. What?

EMMA. Can I have a tenner?

EMMA'S FATHER. Do you want the long answer or the short answer?

EMMA. Ummm, the short answer.

EMMA'S FATHER. No.

EMMA. Ach, Daddy. What was the long answer?

EMMA'S FATHER. Noooo!

EMMA. Please.

EMMA'S FATHER. What do you want a tenner for?

EMMA. I'm not telling you.

EMMA'S FATHER. Drugs, is it?

EMMA. Wise up, Daddy.

EMMA'S FATHER. I haven't a penny to scratch myself with, pet. Here, that's a hard word to spell, isn't it? 'Pet.'

EMMA. Catch yourself on.

EMMA'S FATHER. What, can you spell it, can you?

EMMA. Everybody can spell 'pet', the primary ones can probably spell 'pet'.

EMMA'S FATHER. Go on then, spell it for me.

EMMA. Pet. P – E – T.

EMMA'S FATHER. Tea? Tea, did you say? Thank you very much; I'd love a cup.

Clare's Kitchen

CLARE'S MOTHER. Clare? Is that you? Get in here. Get in here right now.

CLARE. What is it, Mammy?

CLARE'S MOTHER. What is it? What is it? Where have you been to all this time?

CLARE. Playing.

CLARE'S MOTHER. Look at the state of you. Look at your new dress. What were you doing, mud wrestling?

CLARE. No, Mammy, just playing.

CLARE'S MOTHER. For Christ's sake. Why do I bother? Why do me and your father bother buying you nice things if you're going to ruin them, run about looking like a tramp. Staying out, not telling us where you're going. That Emma one's not good for you.

CLARE. No, it's not Emma's fault.

CLARE'S MOTHER. I don't have time, I don't even have time to sort that dress of yours out.

CLARE. Where are you going, Mammy? You're not going out, are you? Are you going out?

CLARE'S MOTHER. Just up to Kathy's.

CLARE. Can I come?

CLARE'S MOTHER. No.

CLARE. Oh please, Mammy, can I come?

CLARE'S MOTHER. No, it's late.

CLARE. There's no school.

CLARE'S MOTHER. I said no.

CLARE. I'm sorry about the dress, really I'm sorry, it won't ever happen again, I promise. Just please let me come. I'll be good. I'll be quiet.

CLARE'S MOTHER. Another time, Clare. I'll see you in the morning.

Emma's Kitchen

EMMA (*shouting*). Mammy! There's a crowd of fellas painting something on the side of the house!

EMMA'S MOTHER. Aye. We have your wonderful fucking father to thank for that. Didn't say a word. Well, apart from 'All right, lads, work away, lads, no bother, boss.' Honest to God, if I was at meself, I'd stick them brushes so far up their holes they'd be choking on them. But naw, oll over and play dead, that's his motto, he'll get a couple of free pints in the pub for that the night, you see. Roll over and play dead.

EMMA. What are they painting, Mammy?

EMMA'S MOTHER. Cù fucking Chulainn.

EMMA. Who's Cù Chulainn?

EMMA'S MOTHER. A nine-foot man in a frock, that's who he is. (*Beat.*) I tell you what, they better not write anything, for they can't spell either. Mary Kennedy got stuck with 'up the rebellies' in big black letters all over her coal shed.

EMMA. Do you want a cup of tea, Mammy?

EMMA'S MOTHER (*suspiciously*). What are you after? Or what have you been up to? You better not have been fighting again, Emma.

EMMA. No, I'm making Daddy a cup anyway.

EMMA'S MOTHER. Fuck! He can drink tea, can he? All these years I thought he'd a fear of cups. I thought that's why he used pint glasses.

EMMA. Ach, Mammy.

EMMA'S MOTHER. 'Ach, Mammy' nothing! Useless aul' bastard.

EMMA. Mammy, Mammy… (*Pause.*) Do we have any spare carpet?

Clare's Living Room

CLARE. I'm going to go to bed now.

CLARE'S FATHER. Is that all you're going to do? Stick your head around the door. Is that how you say goodnight to your father?

CLARE. You're watching something.

CLARE'S FATHER. Get in here. (*Pause.*) Out gallivanting all day again.

CLARE. Sorry, Daddy.

CLARE'S FATHER. Your dress is all dirty.

CLARE. I know.

CLARE'S FATHER. Take it off.

CLARE. I will. I'm going to. I'm going up to bed now.

CLARE'S FATHER. What? And drag muck upstairs too, do you think that's a good idea?

CLARE. No.

CLARE'S FATHER. It's filthy. Look at it. What is it?

CLARE. I know, I'm sorry.

CLARE'S FATHER. Take it off now.

CLARE. But, Daddy...

CLARE'S FATHER. Don't make me get angry with you, Clare. Do as I say.

She does.

CLARE. We bought the red carpet from Dennis.

EMMA. I think her father gave her money.

CLARE. She was really excited. I didn't like it, how it looked, how it felt. In a way, it spoilt it for me. It wasn't the same. I became less interested in the tree house.

I was sitting on my front steps, drawing, when she arrived. I watched her. Moving boxes from an old red car into the abandoned number 14. She was tiny and slim, with long blonde wavy hair, not bright blonde though, it was darker, she had it tied back from her face but some of it escaped, fell down over her narrow brown eyes. Her hands were so full that she was attempting to blow the offending strands away, with no success. And from the look of her complexion she enjoyed sitting out on hot days like that one. It's a little film I can play back. Every detail's there, the dark blue jeans, black top, black heels, her nails painted bright blue and all the silver jewellery – a cross around her neck, several rings on her fingers and one on the second toe of her right foot, lots of bracelets, too many, they made a noise when she moved, a bit like a wind chime. She seemed perfect. Not like the rest of us, all pale-skinned and frizzy-haired. She looked a bit like one of Laura's Barbie dolls. I watched her teetering about, almost folding under the weight she carried, until – eventually giving up – she collapsed on one of the boxes at her doorstep, lit a cigarette and inspected her surroundings. From the safety of my steps, I drew her picture.

Clare's Front Steps

CLARE *watches across the street intently.*

EMMA. Has she come out yet?

CLARE. Not yet.

EMMA. Not yet? For God's sake.

CLARE. We'll wait another couple of minutes. She'll have to come out soon. She'll have to go to the shop or something.

EMMA. Will she send us to the shop for her, do you think?

CLARE. I don't know. Maybe. Probably. We'll have to speak to her first, though.

EMMA (*sighs with boredom*). Did you know Laura says I can't come to her fucking party?

CLARE. Aye.

EMMA. As if I even wanted to go. (*Beat.*) You're not going, are you?

CLARE. Shh!

EMMA. Don't tell me to shh!

A short silence. EMMA *is becoming impatient.*

This is boring.

CLARE. You're calling me boring?

EMMA. No. This. Sitting here. What's the point?

CLARE. Do you not want to see her?

EMMA. What's so brilliant about her? She doesn't seem to do much.

CLARE. Go if you want. See if I care.

EMMA. I might.

CLARE. Go on then. Fuck off. Go.

EMMA. Fuck you. Dick.

CLARE. You're a dick.

Short silence.

EMMA. Do you think she is French?

CLARE. She could be. She looks French.

EMMA. I've never seen a French person before.

CLARE. They look, you know, different.

EMMA. Can I see your drawings?

CLARE. Aye. (*Passes them to her.*) Here.

EMMA. These are class. I wish I could draw. I'm crap at art.

CLARE. Wise up.

EMMA (*looking at drawings*). Aye, she does look different. (*Beat.*) Here, I have an idea. Come on.

CLARE. No, I'll wait, just five more minutes.

EMMA. No, this is good; I know how we can find out who she is.

Outside Mags and Josie's House

MAGS. Dear God, naw! She's not French. Her name's Dervla Murray. Her father owns the bookies. French! Youse are a scream. Aren't they a scream, Josie?

JOSIE. They are, surely, what put that idea into your heads?

EMMA. It was Clare who thought it.

CLARE. It wasn't just me, it was you too.

MAGS. She's dark colouring, right enough.

JOSIE. Them sunbeds probably. They're all on them sunbeds now.

MAGS. French! I can't imagine somebody coming all the way from France to live in this place.

JOSIE. There's nothing wrong with this place.

MAGS. It's hardly France now, is it?

JOSIE. When have you ever been in France? I must have missed that. Did you dander over last night when I was at the bingo, did you?

MAGS. Aye, you're fit enough to go to the bingo, critically ill when I ask you to give the kitchen floor a mop.

JOSIE. That's nothing to do with anything. That's not what we were talking about.

MAGS. What were we talking about?

JOSIE. France.

EMMA. Did you win at the bingo, Josie?

CLARE. No, we were talking about Dervla.

MAGS. Ach, God love her too, you know. She's only a bit of a wain herself…

CLARE. Why 'God love her'? What do you mean, Mags?

MAGS. Ach, it won't be easy for her. Out on her own for the first time. It'll be tough enough on her. I've no experience of it myself but it's hard work bringing up a baby, and on top of that (*Whispers*.) there's no sign of a man there.

CLARE. That was the first we'd heard of the baby.

EMMA. Shannon.

CLARE. We hadn't known about the baby.

EMMA. Wee chubby-faced thing.

CLARE. Nothing like her.

EMMA. Spitting image.

CLARE. Although it's difficult, it's sort of worn away.

EMMA. We were camped outside in our usual spot when we first got a glimpse. I was armed with a deck of cards.

CLARE. In the garden. They were playing.

EMMA. She looked funny. I laughed.

CLARE. So small. Not walking, not crawling, not standing, not falling.

EMMA. It was the same day she took the photos.

CLARE. Just timing really. Time.

EMMA. She took a camera, an old one, her father's. She said he wouldn't miss it.

CLARE. It was her idea. I didn't like going in there. That room, all dark – not even dark, black – and it had this smell, it smelt of dust and coffee. It smelt dirty.

EMMA. That's what he did, you see. Photographs. Weddings, christenings, first communions, confirmations.

CLARE. There was no reason behind it.

EMMA. It had this big lens on it.

CLARE. I don't know what purpose we thought it would have.

EMMA. Meant we could see right into her living room from where we sat.

CLARE. I don't know why. It wasn't my idea, you see.

EMMA. It was a while before we actually spoke. I was fed up with it all. I wanted to just go over and bang on the front door and say, 'Hello, Dervla, would you be wanting anything from the shop? We'll go for you, if you like.' I couldn't see what all the fuss was about half the time. But she wouldn't let me. I think she liked not knowing. I think she liked building her into something she wasn't. We didn't do it my way. We waited. We watched. Time passed.

Emma's Back Yard

EMMA. Joe O'Kane was our next-door neighbour. Everyone
called him Joe Tank, he was built like one. Tank's face and
hands and neck were all scarred, all covered in purple and
red bumps, and his voice was so low it was almost a whisper.
Everyone was afraid of him. Everyone said he burnt his wife
alive. The truth of it is she wasn't very well; she locked
herself in her bedroom with a canister of petrol and a box of
matches. The truth of it is, poor Tank knocked the door
through, pulled her out of the flames, down the stairs and
into the front street, before the fire engine even arrived. It
was too late. She was dead, and the flames left their mark on
him too, his reflection now a constant reminder. Poor aul'
Tank. My ma said he was a gentleman. My ma said you
wouldn't get better. (*Pause*.) Tank kept dogs. Not the type
you stroke and play fetch with, not like Toto. Big long-
limbed proud things, nearly as tall as me and not a pick of
meat on their bones. When he took them walks they all wore
muzzles. My cat Lucky went missing the previous year and
they had always been my prime suspects.

TANK. Here, girl, come here, girl. Good girl. Come over here.
Come over here till Emma sees you.

EMMA. Naw, it's all right, Tank, really. I can see her from here.

TANK. This is Sétanta.

EMMA. That's a nice name. Are they all girls, Tank?

TANK. All mine are. Girls are better.

EMMA. That's what I always say. What does Sétanta eat?

TANK. What does she eat? She eats lots of things. You
wouldn't think it to look at her, they run it off.

EMMA. But say if a kitten got in there accidentally, would she
eat a kitten, do you think?

TANK. A kitten wouldn't be silly enough to come in here.

EMMA. Say it was a stupid kitten.

TANK. It would smell the dogs, it wouldn't put its toe in here.

EMMA. Say it was a really thick kitten that maybe didn't have a sense of smell, would Sétanta have it for her dinner?

TANK. She well might, Emma, she well might.

EMMA. I think that's terrible.

TANK. Ach, it's the natural order, it's the way things are. Do you want to pet her?

EMMA. No, I'm grand.

TANK. She might eat a kitten, she'll not eat you.

EMMA. All right then. (*She pets the dog*.) You can feel her bones.

TANK. But she's beautiful, isn't she?

EMMA. Aye... she's... nice.

TANK. You want to see her run, she runs like the wind. She's been good to me. If you were big enough I'd tell you to put a bet on her, she might be good to you too.

The Street

EMMA. Little did we know the biggest event of the summer was brewing. Poor aul' Mags and Josie were discovering the pitfalls of having a great view of the river. The boys were planting a bomb on the bridge, and their house was selected for the headquarters, lookout and canteen facility of the operation. Somehow the army got wind of it – we were soon crawling with them, they made our whole side vacate their houses. Me and Clare went to the shop for supplies, then came back and sat on the pavement to watch the show. The sun could have split the sky in two, soldiers were offering us a pound for one of our five-pence ice poles, I made quite a bit of money. Of course, my da was out shouting the odds, making a show of himself. Needless to say, he didn't approve of my business transactions.

EMMA'S FATHER. Do not be taking money off them dirty bastards, Emma. You stay away from my wee girl, do you hear me? Dirty bastards. Don't be even talking to them, Emma, I'm warning you now, I'm watching you.

EMMA. Everyone was out. Some people had kitchen chairs, and flasks of tea. Soldiers were running in and out of our houses, in our gardens, on our roofs. The threat of the bomb was now long gone, but there remained the problem of the militant Republicans trapped in the house of two old-aged pensioners. My Aunt Rita was saying the rosary with the legion of Mary; no one led the rosary like my Aunt Rita, such speed, such precision, they would pray Mags and Josie to safety. Tank was holding all five of his dogs on leads, they seemed alert, anxious. Time ticked on. Meanwhile, Mags and Josie had relaxed somewhat into their situation. They were sitting in the middle of their sofa with a large balaclava-clad man on either side of them. Each man with an AK47 in one hand and a cup of tea in the other. All four had already reached the stage of panic, it had now long passed, so they decided to sit down and watch the six o'clock news.

IRA MAN 1. Jesus Christ, but the blacks have it bad in South Africa, don't they?

IRA MAN 2. It's unbelievable, completely unbelievable, it's desperate.

JOSIE. God, aye, my heart goes out.

MAGS. Them poor people. Digestive, boys?

EMMA. Two army men were standing talking outside Tank's house. The dogs were going mental, barking and pulling on their leads. He was trying his best to hold them back and just as my father made his way over to give him some help, Sétanta broke free, and before anyone could think about blinking she was on top of one of the soldiers then bang – (*Pause*.) dead at his feet.

EMMA'S FATHER. Jesus Christ! There's wains everywhere, what are you playing at? The thing was wearing a muzzle. You fucking savages. You animals.

EMMA. None of them answered, everyone was shouting, and pointing to the dead dog and lifting their children into their arms as though they would be next.

RITA. Let's not fight fire with fire. We can't start a riot over a greyhound.

EMMA. I watched Tank pull the rest of his dogs away from the carnage. Poor aul' Tank. They got the IRA men eventually, they made their way in through the attic. Mags was all shaken up with the thought of what could have been, and Josie said she felt sorry for the fellas, she said they were just young and stupid. She said they just made a mistake. Clare was still standing in the middle of the road looking at the dead dog's body. I thought she looked just like Bernadette did in that mad painting.

CLARE. My God, Emma.

EMMA. I know.

CLARE. Look at it.

EMMA. I know, it's terrible.

CLARE. Did you see how quickly it happened?

EMMA. Let's go.

CLARE. Do you not want to touch it?

EMMA. What?

CLARE. To touch it. To see what it feels like.

EMMA. No.

CLARE. Why not?

EMMA. That's disgusting.

CLARE. It's not. Go on, touch it. I dare you.

EMMA. The poor thing's dead, Clare.

CLARE. It's only a dog. It's only a stupid dog. I don't see what the big deal is.

EMMA. I can't believe you said that.

CLARE (*looking across the street*). Shh.

EMMA. No I won't 'shh'.

CLARE. Look.

EMMA. That's a terrible thing to say.

CLARE. It's her.

EMMA. Tank loved that dog.

CLARE. Be quiet. It's her, the girl, Dervla, she's coming over here. She's coming over to see the dead dog.

DERVLA. Sweet Jesus. The poor wee thing. Girls, you shouldn't be standing here. It'll leave you all annoyed.

CLARE. We saw it happen and everything.

DERVLA. My God. Somebody would need to take it away. It can't lie there much longer in this heat.

CLARE. It was all over really quickly.

DERVLA. Whose dog was it?

CLARE. Tank's. He lives in that house there, so he does.

DERVLA. I'm sure he's upset.

CLARE. Probably.

DERVLA. What are your names, girls?

CLARE. I'm Clare and this here's Emma. We're best friends.

DERVLA. Thick as thieves, are you?

CLARE. No, we're not thieves.

DERVLA (*laughs*). I'm Dervla.

CLARE. We knew that already, so we did.

DERVLA. Did you indeed?

CLARE. Aye, Mags told us. Do you know Mags?

DERVLA. Well, I do now. They're celebrities now, her and her sister. I better go. I just left the baby for a second.

CLARE. Wee Shannon. We see her playing sometimes, in the garden.

DERVLA. Wee Shannon, that's right. Do you like babies, girls?

CLARE. We love babies.

DERVLA. I suppose, all wee girls love babies, don't they? Well, if you ever fancy taking her a walk for me, I'd be delighted. Five minutes' peace, you know.

Outside Dervla's House

EMMA. 'We love babies'!

CLARE (*knocking on the door*). Hello.

EMMA. What are you on?

CLARE (*knocking on the door*). Hello.

EMMA. When did we decide that we loved babies?

CLARE. Shut up.

EMMA. She's not in. Come on.

CLARE. She is. She is in. I saw her.

DERVLA *opens the door. She has baby Shannon in her arms.*

DERVLA. Hello, girls. This heat would drive you mad, wouldn't it?

Look, Shannon, look at the big girls. Say hello, Shannon, ach, she's all shy. Isn't your dress beautiful, look at Clare's dress, Shannon, isn't that a pretty dress?

CLARE. It's old. I'm not allowed to wear my new stuff out to play any more. It gets all dirty.

DERVLA. I appreciate you doing this, girls. I really do. It's difficult to get a break, you know, with it just being me and the wee woman. (*To Shannon*.) Will I get your pram? Will I? Will I go and get your pram, wee doll? Are the big girls gonna take you a walk? Are they?

EMMA. We took Shannon for lots of walks.

CLARE. At first we were told...

DERVLA. Stay in the street, won't you, girls, so I can keep an eye.

CLARE. But soon we were asking could we bring her to the park. We thought she'd love it.

EMMA. We said we'd be careful.

CLARE. She did.

EMMA. We were. (*Pause*.) I feel cheated, you know. Dragged in.

The Park

The girls are pushing Shannon on a swing.

CLARE. Do you know what they did last night?

EMMA. Are you still watching?

CLARE (*nods*). Don't tell anyone.

EMMA. I won't.

CLARE. They were dancing.

EMMA. Dancing?

CLARE. In the living room.

EMMA. Just the two of them?

CLARE. Who else?

EMMA. Not proper dancing though, Shannon's too wee.

CLARE. Well, she had her in her arms to start with then she put her down and took her by the hands, they were twirling round and round, she was in stitches.

EMMA. Shannon was?

CLARE. Dervla.

EMMA. Aye, my da used to do that with me. Sometimes he still tries to. State of him.

CLARE. It's great, isn't it? Just them together. I think it's great. It's better like that; you know, they seem dead happy, don't they?

EMMA. I saw Tank today.

CLARE. And, you know, sometimes they just sit, they just sit there and watch the TV and it will just be cartoons; you know, stupid cartoons, the boring ones, the real baby ones, but it doesn't matter, she doesn't care.

EMMA. He was outside looking at the grave.

CLARE. It just looks right, I always think to myself, that looks right. It's a wee picture.

EMMA. Do you listen to anything I say?

CLARE. What did you say?

EMMA. I saw Tank, he was out looking at the grave, he looked sad. Not that you care.

CLARE. The dog! The dog again! No, I don't care. It was only a stupid dog, you never shut up about it. You didn't even like it when it was alive. You said it ripped Lucky to pieces.

EMMA. That's not true. She wants down.

CLARE. What?

EMMA. Shannon, do you want down, doll? (*Lifts her down from the swing.*) There you go. Look, you've got her all upset, shouting like that.

CLARE. I didn't shout. She's tired.

EMMA. Let's take her home. I want to go and see it.

CLARE. What?

EMMA. The grave.

CLARE. Oh, for God's sake. Dogs shouldn't even have graves. It's stupid. Tank's a weirdo.

EMMA. He's really nice, Clare.

CLARE. He's boring and he's old.

EMMA. Well, I want to go round and see it.

CLARE. Why?

EMMA. Why? Why do I need a reason? I always do what you want. All the time. You never even have to ask twice. It's not fair, but it doesn't matter, suit yourself, I'll go on my own. (*To Shannon*.) Come on, wee woman, your mammy'll be wondering where we are.

EMMA. Isn't it funny how one thing leads to another.

CLARE. One night stands out.

EMMA. It could easily have been different.

CLARE. I can see her now.

EMMA. One decision.

CLARE. She'd put the baby to bed.

EMMA. I'm not even sure I remember the right way of it.

CLARE. Someone rang.

EMMA. What I know and what I think I know.

CLARE. She was talking to them for a long time. They were making her angry, making her shout.

EMMA. What's real and what I've been told.

CLARE. And when she was finished.

EMMA. It got all mixed up.

CLARE. When she slammed down the phone.

EMMA. Somewhere. Somehow. Along the way.

CLARE. She started crying, crying so much that she wasn't wiping away the tears but sweeping them away, washing her face with them. It was the type of crying that makes no sound. The type I would do. Alone. In the dark.

Clare's Front Steps

CLARE *is watching something across the street.* EMMA *approaches.*

EMMA (*out of breath*). There you are. I was down at the park looking for you and everything. Right, the bad news is I went to the shop and Dennis says he doesn't have any rope. If he did he said he'd hang himself with it rather than spend another day working in this shithole. The good news is sweet Pete has some and he'll give it to us and put the swing up if we give him a pound. The other bad news is Laura has her eye on the same lamp-post. Now, I have 50p so I just need you to get the other half... come on.

CLARE (*distant*). Look.

EMMA. No time, Clare. This is serious, come on.

CLARE. No, but look. There's a man knocking on Dervla's door. He's been there ages.

EMMA. Big deal. Did you not hear what I said?

CLARE. She's in the house and she's not answering the door.

EMMA. Well... he must be one of them Jehovah Witnesses or something. My ma makes us switch off the TV and hide whenever they call round.

CLARE. But he knows her. He's been calling her name through the letterbox and everything. Who do you think he is?

EMMA. I don't know, I don't care. If we don't move soon Laura is gonna be swinging round our lamp-post. Do you want that to happen? Do you?

Tank's Back Yard

CLARE. There's no dates or anything.

EMMA. What?

CLARE. On the headstone. There's no dates or anything. Usually it says on it. You know, it says the date they were born and the date they died, and then it will say something about Mary or Jesus. Well, all the ones in the cemetery are like that anyway.

EMMA. It must be different for dogs. What should we do now, do you think?

CLARE. I don't know, this was your idea.

EMMA. Should we say a prayer or something?

CLARE. Ach, don't be a dick.

EMMA. Well, I don't know. Here he comes. (*Calling*.) Hi, Tank, we just wanted to call round and you know… pay our respects.

CLARE (*under her breath*). Dick.

EMMA. And see the headstone and that, you can't see it properly from our yard. It's nice, so it is… it's lovely.

TANK. I think it's an eyesore myself.

EMMA. Then why did you buy it, Tank?

TANK. I didn't, you see. They had a whip round in the pub, two fellas knocked on the door with it in their hands, saying that Sétanta was an Irish hero, ach, they were blocked, like. I couldn't turn them away. So I just got landed with it. Don't be saying any of this to your father, Emma, I have a feeling it might have been his idea.

EMMA. My da is simple. He really is simple. At least you have something to remind you of her though, even if it is sort of rotten-looking.

TANK. Oh aye, God aye. It's the thought that counts and all that.

EMMA. You couldn't watch my da, so you couldn't. Everyone says it's terrible. What happened. It is terrible. It's a disgrace.

TANK. Aye, but it happened. It's over now.

EMMA. Are you not angry? I would be so angry.

TANK. I never see the point in getting angry.

EMMA. The man shot your dog in the head, Tank.

TANK. Aye. He made a decision. I think he made the wrong decision, but he made it, he did it, it's done. The mind's a mad thing so it is, girls, and when it's under pressure, when it has to work quickly sometimes it makes mistakes. I've done it myself... my poor wife, Ann Marie. You don't remember her, do you, Emma?

EMMA. No, I was only a baby then. My mammy talks about her though.

TANK. Aye, they were good friends, her and your mother. Always up to no good, so they were. When Ann Marie had her accident, they were all holding me back, your father and them all, and I could feel the heat from downstairs, and I must have knew, I mean, I must have known it was too late, I was being stupid, I mean, Jesus, the heat. But you don't think like that, all I could think was I'm going up there, I'm going up there, and it felt like I had the strength of ten men, and I broke loose and up I went, and well, I mean, they were right, look at me. But what I'm saying is sometimes you're just thrown into a situation and you just react.

EMMA. My mammy's right about you, Tank. You're too good for your own good.

CLARE. Tank told us another story that day, while we sat on the grave drinking cold tea. I can't remember how it started. I mean, I know the story, but how did it start?

EMMA. Once upon a time. No. That wasn't it.

TANK. Many many years ago, back in Celtic times, there lived a noble king. The king's beautiful wife had died giving birth to his only son, he now spent most of his time trying to keep himself busy. He hunted a lot. And for this reason, the king kept many dogs. His most loyal and trusted being a greyhound, called Gellert…

CLARE. Gellert was so special to his master that he was given the great responsibility of guarding the nursery of the king's infant son while he was on the hunt…

EMMA. One day, the king returned to his castle later than usual. He called and called for Gellert but the dog didn't come, so he made his way to the nursery…

CLARE. As the king approached the door, he saw Gellert standing just inside. The room had been wrecked, furniture had been broken, the baby's crib was upturned and the king could see no sign of his son…

EMMA. He looked back at the hound who was now lying panting at his feet; the dog's fangs and lips were stained red…

CLARE. 'God no!' cried the king. 'You monster, you have killed my child!' And he took his sword…

EMMA. And drove it through the animal. Then he heard a faint…

CLARE. Crying coming from the upturned crib. He…

EMMA. Ran to it, and lifted it up…

CLARE. Underneath sat his son, upright, unharmed, and beside him…

EMMA. Lay a slaughtered wolf, dripping with blood.

The Street

CLARE *and* EMMA *are sitting on the pavement playing cards.*

CLARE. Snap.

EMMA. Raging.

They play again.

CLARE. Snap.

EMMA. For God's sake! Raging! Well, I still have more cards, I'm still the winner. You're the *loser*. You're the *loser*! Clare? Clare?

CLARE. Sorry? What?

EMMA. I was just… it doesn't matter. What's wrong with you? You're really quiet.

CLARE. Oh, I'm just thinking.

EMMA. About what?

CLARE. Nothing.

EMMA. Look at us, stuck here playing cards. God, I hate Laura. I hate her. I wish she would just die. She hasn't taken her arse off that swing since her big fatso da put it up for her. She's just doing it to wind us up, you know. Oh, I could kill her. I could just tie her to that lamp-post permanently with her big stupid ringlets and let her dangle from it. Snap. You're not even paying attention to the game now.

CLARE. There's swings in the park. I mean, if you really want a swing.

EMMA. They're crap.

CLARE. Mammy's going away.

Clare's Bedroom

CLARE'S MOTHER. Look at me, Clare. Look at me. You need to pay attention to this. It's a week, right. I'm going to hang them up in order, so you just have to lift them out, you start with this blue dress here and you work your way back. Are you following me, Clare? And then all your hair bobbles are lined up here, on the dresser so they're in the same order as the outfits, right, okay – so that's Monday, Tuesday, Wednesday, and all your underwear is in your top drawer there and your socks. Wear your ankle socks now. Don't be running around in knee socks, they're for school. I hate girls running around in knee socks in the summer. I hope I don't come home and find you've been walking around looking like a tramp. You're a big girl now, this is your responsibility.

The Street

Returning to the card game.

EMMA. Snap! Ha ha! Where's she going?

CLARE. Donegal. With my Aunt Kathy.

EMMA. The mad one.

CLARE. Aye. Mammy says she needs a break.

EMMA. Do you not want her to go?

CLARE. Naw.

EMMA. I know how you feel.

CLARE. Really.

EMMA. Aye, my ma went away for five days one time and my hair never got brushed.

CLARE. I brush my own hair.

EMMA. So do I. Now.

CLARE. Snap.

EMMA. For fuck's sake.

CLARE. You said fuck.

EMMA. You say fuck all the time.

CLARE. I don't.

EMMA. You do. Fuck, fuck, fuck, that's all you say. Snap.

CLARE. I saw the man at Dervla's again. The dark-haired man, the one you thought was a Jehovah's Witness.

EMMA. When?

CLARE. I saw him today, he rapped the door, and then he just went away.

EMMA. That rhymes. You're a poet and you don't know it, ha ha!

CLARE. Who is he, Emma?

EMMA. I don't know.

CLARE. I wish he'd just stop.

EMMA. Guess what?

CLARE. Always knocking. I wish he'd just leave them alone.

EMMA. Laura kicked Connor in the face this morning. Everybody thinks she's so good and so perfect, but she had Connor on the ground and she was kicking the shit out of him. You wanted to see the state of him when she'd finished. Face on him like a butcher's window. There's no need for that, like.

CLARE. You punched Connor in the back yesterday.

EMMA. Ach, Clare, that's not what I'm talking about. I'm not talking about me punching Connor; I'm talking about her being a dick. Come on. Let's go and walk the baby.

The Railings

EMMA. Our lady wept a lot that week. The week her mother
left, it was a miserable one. Pissing with rain but still hot. I
didn't see much of Clare at all, I don't think she was allowed
out, you know, because of the rain. Then I was up tidying my
room – well, you know, pushing things into my cupboard –
and I stopped to look out the window. There she was. Sitting
on the railings at the bottom of the street, on her own, just
sitting there. She was wearing two different socks, it was
obvious they were different as well, one was red and the
other was yellow. I went out to her, I had my father's coat
with me and I held it over both our heads. I didn't ask her
why she was out in the rain, I didn't ask her why she had no
coat on, or why she was wearing two different socks. I just
started talking, I told her about my Aunt Rita, saying she had
this great surprise for me, which turned out to be a statue of
the Virgin Mary that glows in the dark. About me bouncing
on my bed, breaking three springs, and trying to hide the evi-
dence. Sometimes she'd smile or nod, sometimes she would
laugh or say 'Really?' but I don't know if she was listening.
So when I'd ran out of things to tell her, I just sat there,
swinging my legs, beside her, on the railings, in the rain.
Then I saw what she'd been looking at, on the telephone
wires, above the street – rows and rows of birds who'd been
sitting to attention, were beginning to fly away and her eyes
were following them. She watched them moving off into the
distance, and I turned to her and said, 'Do you think they'll
fly over the rainbow?' And she said, 'No, they're not blue-
birds.' But she never took her eyes off them, then she stood
up, she stood up and quietly, almost under her breath said,
'You know, from here, they look just like tiny little pieces of
ash, and the sky, the sky looks like smoke.'

Clare's Front Steps

CLARE. He's been there again. Knocking. I wish he'd just go
away. He was there again, knock-knock-knocking. What
does he want? Go away! Go away and leave her alone.
Patrolling her house, circling it, banging on doors, banging
on windows. Just shut up. Just shut up and go away. He
knows she's in there. He knows it, he can smell her, and he
can wait. She'll have to come out some time, he thinks. So
he sits, he sits and waits and when she does step out, then
he'll pounce.

Outside Mags and Josie's House

MAGS. What do I need now? Hold on a wee minute now, let
me think now, what was it I said I needed?

JOSIE. You wanted eggs. Sure, it's all you've talked about, you
said you're dying for a boiled egg. Jesus, but you're getting
as forgetful.

MAGS. Clare not with you today, Emma love?

EMMA. No, she doesn't want to play today.

MAGS. Ach, there's nothing for you to do anyway I'm sure,
weather like that.

EMMA. Well, me and Marty and Casper are going to the
cinema, so we are. They're showing *The Wizard of Oz* on the
big screen, just for this week, like.

MAGS. That's nice, isn't it, Josie? They're going to the pictures. Isn't that nice?

JOSIE. Ach, that's a great film, they do right; they should show
the old ones all the time, they're far better. That's a great
film, what is it, what is it she sings now... (*Singing*.) 'Follow
the Yellow Brick Road, follow the Yellow Brick Road,
follow, follow, follow...'

MAGS. Ach, for Christ's sake, you'll have the woman turning in her grave.

JOSIE. Is she dead?

MAGS. Aye, I'm nearly sure she's dead, aye.

Clare's Front Steps

CLARE *sits in a daze, looking across the street.* EMMA *approaches.*

EMMA. Clare? Clare?

CLARE *does not respond.*

Me and Marty and Casper are going to the pictures later, you're invited too.

No response.

It's *The Wizard of Oz. The Wizard Of Oz* on the big screen. Imagine! It'll be class. (*Pause.*) Ach, Clare, do what you like. I don't even know what I've done to annoy you. But if you want to sit about feeling sorry for yourself all day that's your problem...

CLARE. She let him in.

EMMA. Who?

CLARE. Dervla. She let him in.

EMMA. Who did she let in?

CLARE. The dark-haired man, the Jehovah Witness man. He's in there. He's in there with her now.

EMMA. Right.

CLARE. They've pulled the curtains. Why would you pull the curtains in the middle of the day?

EMMA. You're not still watching, are you?

CLARE. If you don't want someone to see, that's why you'd do it.

EMMA. Why do you care so much?

CLARE. He's not supposed to be there. It was supposed to be just the two of them. They were happy.

The Cinema

EMMA. I was a bit disappointed with the whole cinema affair. My mother had given us some money. Firstly, Marty and Casper didn't want to come in because...

CASPER. *Wizard of Oz* is for faggots, isn't it, Marty? Isn't it for faggots?

MARTY. Aye, it's for queers.

CASPER. It's for gaylords, so it is.

MARTY. It's all right for you cos you're a girl, we're not sitting in there, not like two gaylords.

CASPER. Aye, we're not sitting in there like two faggot, gaylord, fairy, gay, queers.

MARTY. So just give us the money, give us our cut and don't tell me ma!

EMMA. I ended up sitting through it on my own, I wanted to buy one of them big buckets of popcorn, the ones you see on the TV, but I couldn't afford it. I mean, I didn't even like popcorn, it was just a notion. So I watched it alone and empty-handed. It was still good, like, it was always good. And it was great to see it like that, massive and so loud and it didn't crackle like Dennis's video did. But I had no one to talk about it with afterwards. You've never really seen a film if you don't talk about it. Well, that's what I think.

Dervla's House

CLARE. I want to take the baby a walk.

DERVLA. Not now, Clare love, call back later on.

CLARE. I want to take the baby a walk.

DERVLA. Well, you can't, not now, later maybe.

CLARE. Why not?

DERVLA. She's sleeping, Clare. She's upstairs sleeping.

CLARE. Will I wait here until she wakes up?

DERVLA. No… no… why would you…? She might not wake
up for a while. No, go and play. I'll give you a shout. Go and
play. Where's Emma?

CLARE. I don't know.

DERVLA. Well, go and find her, go on, go and find her, go and
play. You can't keep knocking on my door like this, Clare –
you'll wake Shannon.

CLARE. Then she came back.

EMMA. I shouldn't have.

CLARE. She always came back.

EMMA. I should have kept my distance when she exploded, but
I didn't and there were pieces of her everywhere, pieces of
her all over me. Her mess was all over me. I've never been
able to clean it up.

Clare's Bedroom

CLARE *is sitting on the floor, she is has a basin of water between her legs, a pile of dolls' clothing on her left, and a collection of naked dolls on her right.* EMMA *enters the room.*

CLARE. What are you doing here? How did you get in?

EMMA. It was open, your da's out in the street, he said just to come on up.

CLARE. Well, you'll have to go. I'm too busy. You'll have to go.

EMMA. I'm sick of this. If you don't want to play with me any more, just say it. Just come out and say it.

CLARE. No. I don't mean that. I'm just busy. I'm telling the truth. My mammy's back tomorrow, she's back tomorrow, Emma, and I've nothing done. I need to tidy the whole room, under my bed, everywhere, I need to tidy it all up, and I need to clean. She'll kill me.

EMMA. It looks fine.

CLARE. It's filthy, it's dirty, even these, even these stupid things, they're disgusting. They all need washed. She'll go mad. So you see I have no time, that's all.

EMMA. I'll give you a hand.

CLARE. Okay. Right. Okay. Umm, now hold on, don't touch anything yet, not yet, I want to do them all in order, so that I know – so that I'm sure which ones I've done and which ones I haven't.

EMMA. God, Clare, your mother would have an actual heart attack if she lived in our house. Our Marty's a dirty bastard. (*Examining a doll she has in her hand.*) Clare, I can't put this one in.

CLARE. Aye, you can.

EMMA. No, look, it has a battery part at the back, it'll get ruined.

CLARE. I want her washed, I want all of them clean, it doesn't matter if the stupid thing doesn't work, I never play with it. As long as it looks okay, it doesn't matter if it's broken, it just sits there, it just sits there and gets looks at.

EMMA. You a mentalist, pure mad, but if that's what you want. (*Immerses the doll in water.*) So you found out who the man was then?

CLARE. What man?

EMMA. What man! The Jehovah Witness man. The man who's been in Dervla's. The man you haven't shut up about.

CLARE. No, how did I? What makes you think that?

EMMA. Oh, he's out talking to your da.

CLARE. In the street?

EMMA. Aye.

CLARE. What? Now? (*Running to window.*) Where?

EMMA. They're all standing at Dervla's front door – him, her, your da, Shannon.

CLARE. No they're not, I can't see them.

EMMA. They were. Must be finished talking now.

CLARE. I can't believe you didn't tell me.

EMMA. I did tell you.

CLARE. Sooner.

EMMA. Sorry, I thought you knew. I thought you were behind it.

CLARE. Behind what?

EMMA. Well, he… the man, I mean, he was getting a price from your da. He wants photos of Shannon, he wants a big one for the living room, well, that's what he was saying.

CLARE. For Dervla's living room.

EMMA. Aye.

CLARE. He wants a photo of Shannon for Dervla's living room.

EMMA. Aye.

CLARE. And what did she say?

EMMA. Dervla, nothing, she was just smiling.

CLARE. Why is he sorting out photos of Shannon, what has it got to do with him? He's nobody, he's a stranger.

EMMA. Oh, wise up, Clare.

CLARE. What?

EMMA. You're meant to be the smart one. He's hardly a stranger now. I mean, it's obvious who he must be.

CLARE. Who?

EMMA. Well, he must be Shannon's daddy.

CLARE. This is where I stop. Usually it will all wrap up somewhere around here. There's no word I can find for this, you see, sometimes there just isn't a word – it's not anger not fear not sadness not regret not anything. It's never come that far, because I get the desire, you see, to just push both my hands against my face, to dig into the flesh with my nails, rip it open, and pull all the contents out. So I stop. I forget. (*Pause.*) It was late, and it was dark and I was in my room, all alone, all over now, with the smell still everywhere. I could never sleep after a nightmare. My mother would be back soon; it wouldn't matter so much then. I know what I should have done. I should have screamed and cried, I should have broken, shattered, I should have tore things up and down, I should have made noise, I should have opened my mouth and let all the noise, any noise just stream out. And it did rise up in me, it went right up through my gut, across my chest and into my throat, but it would get lodged there, get stuck, it never did reach my mouth, my lips, it just slowly slid back down, then the threat was over, it settled, subsided, rested. (*Pause.*) I pulled a chair up to my window and opened it wide. I wanted some air. Across the street her light was on, the curtains were

pulled but her light was still on. She never did call me, you
see. She said she would call me and I could walk the baby but
she never did. I waited and waited all day, but no, there were
other things, other new exciting things, it slipped her mind. I
couldn't believe it, I just kept thinking about it – him turning
up out of nowhere and the next thing in the house late at night,
curtains drawn deciding where he'll hang his new photograph.
And I'm putting on my shoes, I'm creeping down the stairs,
out the door and I don't know why, I never stop to think. I just
want to go to her house, just to be there, and it's so quiet, it's a
ghost town, and here I am standing in my white nightdress and
my black shoes, my good black patent shoes, standing at her
front steps. And her window, there was a gap, just a little one,
but enough to have a look, and I needed to and this would be
the last time, this would be the very last time. So I did, I
looked, I knelt down, and I looked. I wish I hadn't. There they
were, both of them, lying on the sofa – well, she was, he
wasn't, he was lying on her, pushing down on her, one hand in
her top and the other up her skirt, grabbing and pushing and
pawing and all the time slobbering, slabbering all over her, as
if it wasn't bad enough, as if she needed his breath on her. He
didn't care though, did he? They don't, do they? He just
carried on, all fat and sweat and red. And then her skirt started
moving up, you see, sliding up, and for a minute I couldn't
work it out – because he hadn't stopped what he was doing,
but then I saw what it was, it was her, it was her doing it
herself, pulling her own skirt up, up over her hips and then she
was tugging at his belt, you know, opening it. She was.
Herself. And my head was melting, you know, my head was
spinning. I mean, I was thinking, why would she, why would
she want to do that – to get it over, to have it finished, maybe,
to end it quickly, you know, like pulling a plaster off or something and I did it without thinking, I made a fist with my right
hand and banged it on the window, once and it stayed there,
my hand on the window. He didn't hear it, but she turned her
head, slightly. I mean, she hardly moved at all but it was
enough, enough to see me standing there, watching, and it was
just like when the blood was pissing out of that dog, I was

fixed, I wanted to run but I didn't, I was just looking at her, I mean, it could only have been a few seconds – her face turned grey, like she was sick, like she was about to vomit, and I knew what she thought of me, because I thought it myself. Then I turned on my heel, I ran.

The Street

EMMA *is throwing a ball against the curb of the pavement.*

EMMA. Fuck her!

CLARE. It's not a big deal, Emma, really.

EMMA. No, fuck her! The fucking bitch. We were doing her a favour, you know, we were helping. I hated taking the thing out anyway, all she did was cry. But to see Laura pushing her about, that's not on. Laura pushing her about looking all clever, as if to say, 'This used to be your job, didn't it? But you weren't good enough.' I'm going to hit that Laura such a dig.

CLARE. It's not Laura's fault.

EMMA. Everything is Laura's fault, she probably told her about us smoking that time, that *one time*. I'm going to kill her. First she takes our swing, then our wain. Fucking bitch!

CLARE. It's nothing to do with Laura; it's the man, Shannon's daddy. Dervla said he doesn't like us.

EMMA. Why does he not like us? What the fuck is there not to like about us?

CLARE. I don't know. That's just what she said. Maybe he saw you fighting or something.

EMMA. Don't blame me.

CLARE. I'm not. Let's forget it now.

EMMA. When were you talking to her?

CLARE. Who?

EMMA. Dervla, when did she tell you all this?

CLARE. Today.

EMMA. What time today?

CLARE. God, I don't know, earlier. (*Defensive*.) I'm not lying.

EMMA. I mean, you should have seen her down there, swinging Shannon about like a rag doll, as if the wain would even enjoy that, why didn't she just take her to the park? She's doing it so we see her, it's all for show. I'm going to say something to Dervla as well. I mean, we haven't even done anything wrong, for once; I'm going to ask what's going on. I might do it now; aye, I'm going to ask her now.

CLARE. No, don't, please don't.

EMMA. Why not?

CLARE. You can't.

EMMA. Why? Why can I not?

CLARE. You're all angry; you're all worked up.

EMMA. I don't care. I have done nothing wrong, and now she's deciding I'm not good enough to take her fucking stupid baby a walk, when I've been doing it all this time – we've been doing it all this time

CLARE. You're not going to talk to her.

EMMA. Aye, like you'll stop me.

CLARE. You'll show yourself up.

EMMA. And what?

CLARE. You're not going. It's over, I've told you what happened, you don't need to.

EMMA. I'll decide for myself.

EMMA *attempts to walk away but* CLARE *pulls her back*.

Let go of me.

CLARE. Just listen.

EMMA. Let go.

CLARE. I need you to do what I'm telling you.

EMMA. What do you think you're doing – I said leave me, you fucking weirdo, you psycho.

CLARE takes hold of EMMA*'s hair pulls but then releases her, as though changing her mind.*

Why didn't you hit me?

CLARE. I don't want to hit you.

Short silence.

EMMA. We went our separate ways, without even talking about it, it was just instinctive, you know. I mean, usually when things got a bit heated, fifteen minutes apart would solve it, fifteen minutes and we'd miss each other, we'd be friends again.

CLARE. She left the street.

EMMA. I went to the park. I remember that, and people saw me there. I was in the park.

CLARE. And I had planned to say something. I don't know, to apologise or something. Only now it was more urgent but when I reach the house, the front door's open and she, the baby, Shannon, is sitting in the garden with some toys, you know, those big jigsaw things. Sitting on this wee blue blanket.

EMMA. And then suddenly.

CLARE. All on her own on her wee blue blanket.

EMMA. She turned up.

CLARE. Hello, wee doll.

EMMA. I was surprised.

CLARE. It was done.

EMMA. She had Shannon by the hand.

CLARE. I told her we'd take her to see the tree house.

EMMA. But I don't understand.

CLARE. It's fine. It's sorted.

EMMA. How? What happened?

CLARE. I thought you'd be happy.

EMMA. I am, of course I am.

CLARE. I told her we'd take her to see the tree house. Are you coming?

EMMA. Yeah, I'll come. I'll come to the tree house.

The Journey to the Tree House

CLARE. You searched in your pocket and you said, 'Now, let's see, what do we have here?' and produced a lollipop for her.

EMMA. A bright blue lollipop.

CLARE. A bright yellow lollipop, and her face was dancing and her chubby wee hands couldn't get the wrapper off, so I did it for her and you said…

EMMA. There you go, wee woman, that's better, isn't it?

CLARE. Do you remember that?

EMMA. The shortcut we'd used before was all blocked up.

CLARE. Bonfire wood covered the entrance, we couldn't move it.

EMMA. I think she got a splinter.

CLARE. Meant we had to go the long way, the way Pete had shown us, a lifetime ago.

EMMA. Seemed even further.

CLARE. Then it started to rain again.

EMMA. Made matters worse, pouring down, and we weren't really sure where we were going any more.

CLARE. Or what we were doing.

EMMA. Or why we were doing it. But the situation was there, created, and I was in it and I just kept moving on, walking forward.

CLARE. We took turns carrying her for a while.

EMMA. I tried to pull her wee jumper up over her head so she wouldn't get wet.

CLARE. But we were tired.

EMMA. I took her hand to let her walk.

CLARE. Getting there was the most important thing.

EMMA. To be dry.

CLARE. To be safe.

EMMA. So I was kind of like – dragging her along, you know, by the arm, she was so slow.

CLARE. She started crying.

EMMA. Her legs were all red, you see.

CLARE. When I looked back they'd both stopped, they'd both stopped moving.

EMMA. From the stinging nettles.

CLARE. Emma, why are you just standing there? Why is she crying?

EMMA. She's hurt her legs, her legs are all sore.

CLARE. Then pick her up, pick her up and come on.

EMMA. Maybe we should go back.

CLARE. No, we can't.

EMMA. The rain, Clare.

CLARE. We can't, not now, anyway we're nearly there.

EMMA (*to Shannon*). Shh, doll, we're nearly there, then you'll see the big tree house, you'll like that.

She didn't want to go up the ladder.

CLARE. I thought we could just stay there for a while.

EMMA. It was scary I suppose.

CLARE. Just the three of us.

EMMA. So high off the ground.

CLARE. Emma lifted her up.

EMMA. Clare took her in her arms.

CLARE (*to Shannon*). There we go, it's all over now, it's finished now. Look, look where you are. This is nice, isn't it? Shh, you can shh now.

EMMA. It wasn't nice, it was damp, and we were all wet, the tree house looked like shit without the help of the sun.

CLARE. And it never crossed my mind that the worrying had already started, and had transformed itself to panic. It began almost as soon as the rain did, when Dervla ran outside to bring her daughter in from playing, into the shelter, into the heat – only to find she'd vanished, she'd gone.

EMMA. Soon the whole street were out, looking, searching, saying it would be all right, saying she'd just wandered off, children wander off.

CLARE. Everyone sick to the stomach, some thinking the worst, some thinking of strangers and bad men, but there were none, there was only us. She wouldn't look at anything, I wanted her to see but she wouldn't look at anything.

EMMA. She was crying so much, not listening and her breathing was all funny, her nose was running down into her mouth, her face was purple.

CLARE. Just sitting there rambling, just nonsense, you know, not real words.

EMMA. Shh.

CLARE. Why won't she shut up?

EMMA. Shh.

CLARE. I needed her to be quiet, just for a second.

EMMA. Shh.

CLARE. This was all so we could be there, the three of us, together, all high up, all safe, but it was spoilt. I took her to show her, I don't know – to make her happy, to make us happy, but she was screaming. And the rain thumping down, and her screaming and I knew they'd think I was bad.

EMMA. I didn't hit her.

CLARE. Shut up.

EMMA. It wasn't me. I didn't hit the baby.

CLARE. Just shut the fuck up.

EMMA. I wanted to take her back.

CLARE. No. She never once said that.

EMMA. How can she cry so much?

CLARE. What is wrong with you? Stop it.

EMMA. Nothing worked, you know, not lifting her, not nursing her...

CLARE. Stop it, stop fucking crying.

EMMA. She just wants her mammy.

CLARE. Well, she's not here. (*To Shannon.*) Your mammy's not here, is she? So shut the fuck up.

CLARE *picks Shannon up, keeping her at arm's length, moving to the edge of the tree house, holding her over it.*

EMMA. Give her to me.

CLARE. No.

EMMA. Give her to me.

CLARE. Look, Shannon, look down there, do what I'm telling you, look down, do as I say. Look. I said look.

EMMA. Close your eyes.

CLARE. Are you stupid? Just be quiet, just shut your fucking mouth.

EMMA. Close your wee eyes.

CLARE. I can do it too –

She screams, and continues to scream until she runs out of breath. She shakes Shannon violently.

Stop it! Stop it! Stop it!

EMMA. Then, as quickly as it started.

CLARE. I let go.

EMMA. It was over.

CLARE. Let her slip through my hands.

EMMA. As easy as that.

CLARE. It ended.

EMMA. She was just lying there. In the muck.

CLARE. Conclude, finish, cease.

EMMA. She could have been sleeping.

CLARE. Stop, halt, close.

EMMA. I thought she might move.

CLARE. To end.

EMMA. She didn't.

CLARE. It's okay.

EMMA. We couldn't even see any blood.

CLARE. She wandered off.

EMMA. We wrapped her in the red carpet, we pulled it from the tree house – it was so wet and heavy.

CLARE. She wandered off herself and fell.

EMMA. Then we covered her with leaves. We ran.

CLARE. Still running.

EMMA. It didn't take them long.

CLARE. They soon slotted the big clumsy Jigsaw pieces together.

EMMA. A matter of hours really.

CLARE. They knew, they found her.

EMMA. Asking me just to tell the truth, just tell the truth and everything would be all right.

CLARE. They didn't want the truth.

EMMA. They waited with their breath held and their pencils sharpened.

CLARE. They wanted a bogeyman, they wanted a wolf.

EMMA. I don't think I ever gave the right answers.

CLARE. Instead they got me. Me, I'm the monster.

EMMA. I'll imagine what she looks like now.

CLARE. And it's never quiet.

EMMA. Or what she does.

CLARE. It's never quiet any more.

EMMA. Or how she speaks.

CLARE. I had my dream again.

EMMA. I'm forever finding questions.

CLARE. I'm standing in the street.

EMMA. And I'll think, maybe Clare knows, maybe Clare knows, because I don't.

CLARE. We both are.